ENDANGERED ANIMALS AROUND THE WORLD

ENDANGERED INVERTEBRATES AROUND THE WORLD

BY GOLRIZ GOLKAR

PEBBLE
a capstone imprint

Published by Pebble, an imprint of Capstone
1710 Roe Crest Drive, North Mankato, Minnesota 56003
capstonepub.com

Copyright © 2025 by Capstone. All rights reserved. No part of this publication may be reproduced in whole or in part, or stored in a retrieval system, or transmitted in any form or by any means, electronic, mechanical, photocopying, recording, or otherwise, without written permission of the publisher.

Library of Congress Cataloging-in-Publication Data is available on the Library of Congress website.

ISBN: 9780756578367 (hardcover)
ISBN: 9780756578756 (paperback)
ISBN: 9780756578763 (ebook PDF)

Summary: From spotted butterflies to sand-dwelling beetles, these endangered invertebrates are having a tough time. Learn about some incredible invertebrates that need our help to survive.

Editorial Credits
Editor: Ericka Smith; Designer: Sarah Bennett; Media Researcher: Svetlana Zhurkin; Production Specialist: Katy LaVigne

Image Credits
Alamy: agefotostock, 22; Andrew Cannizzaro: 16; Dreamstime: Jillian Cain, 27; Getty Images: Created by drcooke, 15, Ed Reschke, 11, imageBROKER/Bernd Zoller, 23, Joe McDonald, 19, Michal Fuglevic, 21, milehightraveler, 12; Shutterstock: asantosg, 7, Dean Clarke, 29, Jim Schwabel, 26, kan_khampanya, 9, Marina Poushkina, 14, MarksPursuit, 13, Martha Marks, 17, Melody Mellinger, 4, Ondrej Prosicky, cover, RLS Photo, 5, ungvar, 6, Viacheslav Lopatin, 1; U.S. Fish and Wildlife Service: 25, Ayla Skorupa, 18; USGS: Joe Giersch, 8, 10

Any additional websites and resources referenced in this book are not maintained, authorized, or sponsored by Capstone. All product and company names are trademarks™ or registered® trademarks of their respective holders.

TABLE OF CONTENTS

All About Endangered Invertebrates 4
Mist Forestfly 8
Coral Pink Sand Dunes Tiger Beetle 12
Noel's Amphipod 16
Brook Floater 18
Apollo Butterfly 20
Making Progress 24
How You Can Help 28

    Glossary 30
    Read More 31
    Internet Sites 31
    Index 32
    About the Author 32

Words in **bold** are in the glossary.

All About Endangered Invertebrates

What Are Invertebrates?

A butterfly lands on a flower. It drinks some nectar. *Yum!* Butterflies are invertebrates.

Invertebrates have no backbone. Some have soft bodies. Some have shells. Others have a hard covering. It's called an **exoskeleton**. A few invertebrates have rough, spiny skin.

There are about 1.2 million known **species** of invertebrates. They include insects, spiders, **mollusks**, jellyfish, starfish, worms, and **crustaceans**. But there are millions more that have not been named! They are found all over the world.

What Is an Endangered Invertebrate?

About one in five species of invertebrates is **endangered**. There are not many of them alive. They may become **extinct**.

Invertebrates are endangered for many reasons. **Climate change** is making some of their **habitats** too warm to live in. Farming and construction destroy their homes. And pollution makes them sick.

Where Do Endangered Invertebrates Live?

Endangered invertebrates live all over the world. Many are found in North America.

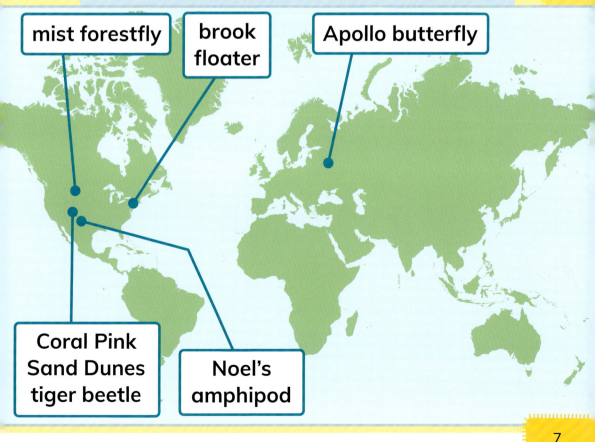

Here's where you can find the invertebrates you'll learn about in this book!

mist forestfly

brook floater

Apollo butterfly

Coral Pink Sand Dunes tiger beetle

Noel's amphipod

Mist Forestfly

A mist forestfly buzzes near a stream. It lands on a rock and takes a drink. The icy water is the melted snow from nearby glaciers.

Glacier National Park

Mist forestflies are only found in one place. They live in Glacier National Park in Montana. They need very cold water to survive. But the glaciers are melting too fast because of climate change. The glaciers may disappear by 2030.

The mist forestfly is endangered. Without glaciers, it will lose its habitat and die. Groups are teaching people about slowing down climate change to try to help.

A young mist forestfly

Glaciers melting in Glacier National Park

Coral Pink Sand Dunes Tiger Beetle

A tiger beetle hides in a sand burrow. *Bam!* It grabs an insect and pulls it inside. It's lunchtime!

Tiger beetles are found all over the world. More than 100 species live in North America. But this one is different. It only lives in Utah's Coral Pink Sand Dunes State Park.

Coral Pink Sand Dunes State Park

This beetle's small population is endangered. Drought is a major problem. Beetle **larvae** die from thirst. The sand dries up too. And beetles have trouble digging burrows.

Vehicles crush adult beetles and plants. The beetle's **prey**, like flies and spiders, need plants to survive. Without enough food, the beetles slowly starve.

Some people are working to protect the beetle. They ask people not to drive in the park.

Barriers keep people away from parts of the park.

Noel's Amphipod

The Noel's amphipod is a crustacean. It lives in shallow, cool, and oxygen-rich waters.

Noel's amphipods were once found in several parts of New Mexico. But people pumped water out of their habitats. Now they are only found near Bitter Lake. Fires burned plants that gave them shade. They cannot survive in sunlight. And oil and gas drilling can pollute their waters.

The Noel's amphipod's habitat in Bitter Lake National Wildlife Refuge

Since 2005, Noel's amphipod has been protected by the United States government. People are working to reduce water pumping and pollution.

Brook Floater

About 7 out of 10 of all mussel species are endangered. The brook floater is one of them. It lives in East Coast streams and rivers.

Brook floaters face many problems. Construction can add soil to the waters they live in. This pollutes their homes.

Predators are also a big issue. Raccoons, muskrats, and otters eat brook floaters.

People are trying to protect mussel habitats from construction. It is also illegal to bring other fish to their habitat. This helps keep predators away.

Apollo Butterfly

An Apollo butterfly flutters through a meadow. Its black and white wings have big orange spots.

Apollo butterflies are endangered in some parts of Europe. Construction and farming are destroying plants and flowers they need to live. Apollo caterpillars eat plants. And adults drink flower nectar.

People pumped water from the wetlands nearby. They plant flowers that don't normally grow there. The butterflies don't like the plants.

Some people are helping Apollo butterflies. They are protecting areas where Apollo butterflies **breed**. This helps the caterpillars grow into butterflies.

Apollo caterpillars

They also protect feeding areas. They make sure the butterflies have food.

Some people are even breeding Apollo butterflies and releasing them in the wild.

Making Progress

Morro Shoulderband Snail

The Morro shoulderband snail is only found in central California. It is an important invertebrate. It feeds on decaying plants. This cleans up the environment. This snail also provides food for other animals.

This snail became endangered in 1994. Only a few hundred were left in the wild. People were building on the land. They destroyed the snail's habitat.

Groups worked to protect the snail. They planted the dune scrub plants this snail likes to live on. By 2022, this snail was no longer endangered.

Atala Butterfly

Atala butterflies are **native** to Florida, Cuba, the Cayman Islands, and the Bahamas. In the late 1800s, there were many Atala butterflies in the wild.

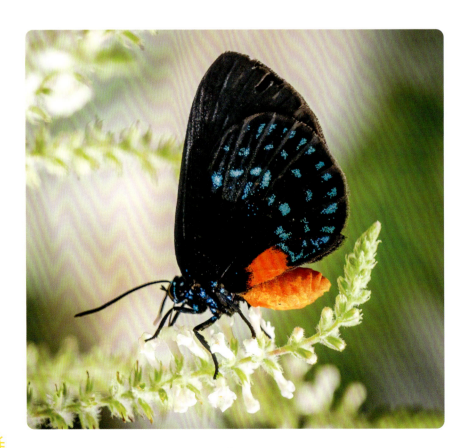

By the 1920s, the coontie plants that Atala caterpillars eat were disappearing. People were using their roots for food. By 1950, Atala butterflies were almost extinct.

Groups helped plant more coontie plants. People grew them in their gardens. By 2019, the butterflies were back!

How You Can Help

Endangered invertebrates need help to survive. Here's what you can do:

» Don't use chemicals in your home. They can pollute waters where invertebrates live.

» Grow plants in your garden that snails and butterflies like.

» Don't remove native plants.

» Spread the word!

GLOSSARY

breed (BREED)—to mate and produce young

climate change (KLY-muht CHAYNJ)—a significant change in Earth's climate over a period of time

crustacean (kruh-STAY-shuhn)—a sea animal with an outer skeleton, such as a crab, lobster, or shrimp

endangered (en-DAYN-juhrd)—at risk of dying out

exoskeleton (ek-soh-SKEH-luh-tuhn)—the hard outer shell of an insect

extinct (ek-STINGKT)—no longer living

habitat (HAB-uh-tat)—the home of a plant or animal

larva (LAR-vuh)—an insect at the stage between an egg and an adult; more than one are called larvae

mollusk (MOL-usk)—a soft-bodied creature that usually has a shell

native (NAY-tuhv)—growing or living naturally in a particular place

prey (PRAY)—an animal hunted by another for food

species (SPEE-sheez)—a group of plants or animals that share common characteristics

READ MORE

Amstutz, Lisa J. *Fast Facts About Butterflies.* North Mankato, MN: Capstone, 2021.

Jaycox, Jaclyn. *Unusual Life Cycles of Invertebrates.* North Mankato, MN: Capstone, 2021.

Morgan, Sally. *Discover It Yourself: Invertebrates.* New York: Kingfisher, 2022.

INTERNET SITES

Kiddle: Invertebrate Facts for Kids
kids.kiddle.co/Invertebrate

National Geographic Kids: Endangered Species Act
kids.nationalgeographic.com/history/article/endangered-species-act

National Geographic Kids: Invertebrates
kids.nationalgeographic.com/animals/invertebrates

INDEX

Apollo butterflies, 7, 20–23
Atala butterflies, 26–27

Bahamas, 26
Bitter Lake, 16
Bitter Lake National Wildlife Refuge, 17
brook floaters, 7, 18–19

California, 24
Cayman Islands, 26
climate change, 6, 9, 10
Coral Pink Sand Dunes State Park, 12, 13
Coral Pink Sand Dunes tiger beetles, 7, 12–15
Cuba, 26

East Coast, 18
Europe, 20

Florida, 26

Glacier National Park, 9, 11

mist forestflies, 7, 8–11
Montana, 9
Morro shoulderband snails, 24–25

New Mexico, 16
Noel's amphipods, 7, 16–17
North America, 7, 12

Utah, 12

ABOUT THE AUTHOR

Golriz Golkar is the author of more than 70 books for children. A former elementary school teacher, she holds degrees in American literature and literacy education. Golriz enjoys reading, cooking, singing with her daughter, and looking for ladybugs on nature walks.